JEWISH ART

JEWISH ART

From the Bible to Chagall

by Ludwig Gutfeld

Translated from the German by
William Wolf

Thomas Yoseloff
New York • South Brunswick • London

6183
Printed in the United States of America

FOREWORD

This book does not claim to be a scientific work of research. It is merely conceived as an art book, which intends to introduce those who are interested in art into the artistic creations of the Jews from the Biblical times to our own. For this reason we have intentionally refrained from adding scientific explanations of the art objects, which speak for themselves.

Jewish art is frequently connected with religion and its rites. Therefore we have explained the origin and the usage of the various objects in the text, which we have deliberately held to a minimum.

The work consists of four sections:

The first part is called "From the World of the Bible," and it grants the reader an insight in Jewish art from patriarchal times to the Bar Kochba rebellion.

The second part, "Art and Writing," is meant to explain Jewish scriptures of various times.

The third part, "Art and Worship," deals with the beauty and the rich forms of sacral objects.

The fourth and last section, "Painting," will reveal the completeness and manysidedness of Jewish creation in this field. Many productions illustrate the work of Jewish artists, from the mosaics and frescoes of ancient synagogues to Israel's modern painters.

We hope that this book will cause our readers to delve into Jewish art.

CONTENTS

JEWISH ART

1

FROM THE WORLD OF THE BIBLE

"Now the Lord said unto Abram: Get thee out of thy country, and from thy kindred, and from thy father's house, unto the land that I will show thee." (Genesis 12:1). It was in the first half of the second millennium before Christ that this call went out to the tribal father of the people of Israel. God had promised him a country, Palestine or Canaan, situated between the two great civilized countries of the ancient Orient, Egypt and Babylonia. It was approximately in the year 2000 B.C. that many peoples migrated through that country, which became the scene of many battles. It was certainly not easy to live and to develop there. The land was open to cultural influences as well as to hostile armies.

During the seventeenth century B.C. Jacob migrated to Egypt. At that time Canaan was a highly civilized country, which consisted of many city states. Egyptian documents prove that between 1600 and 1300 and in the subsequent late-Canaanite period Palestine was ruled by Egyptians.

In the thirteenth century Moses led his people out of Egypt, back into the land of Abraham. The Bible describes the struggles of the Children of Israel with the Canaanites. These battles were fought in many places, and eventually, through conquests and treaties, the people acquired a dwelling place. For a long time they lived in a peaceful coexistence with the Canaanites. Later on the Israelites conquered several Canaanite cities, Hazor in the North for example. Israeli archeologists of modern times have made excavations to confirm this.

In the twelfth century offshoots of the great Aegean migration swept over Canaan. These people, who were finally stopped in Egypt, are called Phoenicians by the Egyptian sources. They are known to us from Roman history.

In Canaan the Children of Israel were constantly warring against the polytheism of the Canaanites and the Philistines, who frequently invaded the country. Nevertheless the Israelites knew how to maintain their spiritual and physical existence.

The Bible tells us how nomad groups, who had only loose connections with each other, developed into a state under one administration. This ascent was the work of the first three kings, and King Solomon put the final touch to it by building the Temple in the capital city of Jerusalem. Thus the unified and sedentary people received a political and religious center. After Solomon's death his realm was divided into two monarchies: Judah with capital of Jerusalem in the South, and in the North the State of Israel, whose kings ruled in the capital city of Samaria.

One hundred and fifty years later King Nebuchadnezzar of Assyria destroyed Israel. For a short while Judah was safe, but in the year 586 B.C. it was conquered by the Babylonians, who destroyed the Temple, removed all of its sacred vessels and exiled the Children of Israel.

Forty years after the destruction of the Temple the Persians under Cyrus conquered many parts of Asia, among them Palestine. In 563 he permitted the Israelites to return to their country and to rebuild the Temple. That structure, completed in 560, was later renewed by King Herod.

In the year 323 Alexander the Great made an end to the rule of the Persians. Conquering Egypt, he also became the ruler of Palestine. Under his generals, who divided the country among themselves, the people of Israel lived in constant restlessness.

In 320 Palestine came under the rules of the Ptolomeans. Their King Ptolomaeus Philadelphus tolerated the Jewish religion and he even had the Bible translated into Greek. But all this changed when, in 198 B.C., the Seleucids followed the Ptolomeans. The Jewish religion was persecuted vehemently, and it was not until 146 B.C., when the Maccabees under Judah Maccabee had conquered Jerusalem, that the Temple service was restored. After his death the Maccabees succeeded in seeing the State recognized. During the Parthian wars — 66 to 33 B.C. — Judah was ruled by the Romans, but in 66 A.D. the Jews revolted against the Roman rulership and regained the country with Jerusalem as its capital. At that time autonomous coins were minted. In the year 70 A.D. Titus besieged the city of Jerusalem and destroyed the Temple. Sixty-five years later the Jews, with Bar Kochba as their leader, revolted again against the Romans, for they had been advised that Emperor Hadrian planned to erect a pagan temple at the spot where their own Temple had stood. In spite of initial successes the Jews had to yield to the mightier power, and their situation was worse than before. After 135 no Jew was allowed to live in Jerusalem.

Encountering different cultural forms is of course reflected in art. It was important to protect oneself against the influence of alien religions. Such a protective measure was the commandment of the decalogue: "Thou salt not make to thyself an image." Thus the idols of the neighboring and hostile nations were not copied, and for a long time the sculpture and the painting of the Jewish people did not have any human images.

From the beginning the art of the Israelites was not *l'art pour l'art*, but rather a handmaiden to religion. According to the Bible, the artists Bezalel and Oholiab, who manufactured the vessels for the sanctuary which was carried ahead of the people during their wanderings through the wilderness, were masters inspired by God.

Modern Israeli archeologists have made their excavations with the Bible in their hand. There they found proofs not only of Jewish art but also of that of other nations.

Canaan must have already been a religious country even before the conquest by the Israelites. This is testified to by the great number of amulets and figurines found through excavations.

The outstanding place of excavation for the products of Egyptian art is Beth Shean. Relics of a vast Egyptian temple and small Egyptian statues reveal to us the worship of Egyptian divinities. Gezer and Megiddo, too, are important. In Megiddo ointment jars were found, made of faïence and having animal shapes. Faïence ducks and doves are typical of Egyptian art. Then there are a great number of round, small bricks — imitations of the

12

holy scarab beetle. They too are mostly of faïence. Frequently the names of kings are inscribed below.

The Bible and Homer consider Phoenician art the best of its time. It spread from Assyria to Greece and France. All Oriental styles are mixed in that art. There we find stylized rings, griffins and lions and Egyptian demons, also female deities with plant stems. These figures of Astarte have been excavated in great numbers. Besides naked idols there is also the image of the same goddess, her hands clasping her breasts. Most probably the oldest Astarte images of Palestine had been already created in Canaanite times before the Children of Israel entered the country.

In Palestine too mixed creatures were known — those Phoenician animal fantasies. Thus in Megiddo an oval-form signet was found, shaped of white chalk, and representing such a fabulous creature. In the same city a ruin reveals architectural creativity. That structure was certainly a masterly creation. A pillared capital makes us assume that it was quite elegantly furnished. Two volutes connected by a triangle, mark it as the successor to the Egyptian form and the forerunner of the Ionic capital of Greece.

Strangely enough, ornamented vessels are rare in Phoenician times. A censer made of chalk has been found in Megiddo. It is surrounded by a wreath of open and closed lotus flowers. It is borne by a stem which is crowned by leaves hanging downward.

Under Alexander the Great Greek art entered the conquered countries. But the East did not just take this art over; it created a Greek style, in which architecture and the art of the ornament gain a victory over logic.

To Judaism the Greek spirit was a pagan one. The Jews' objection to pagan religion was at the same time an objection to its art. At no other time did Jewish art avoid pictures and sculptures as much as at this one. At the same time the unsafe political situation was unfavorable to art. There were no sponsors. The Temple was poorer than ever. Those who administered the State and the Temple were busy defending what they had. Great achievements were only made in the field of small arts. Now the coins of the Maccabees were created. Here for the first time the inclination towards symbolism was visible, an inclination which was to remain with Jewish art.

The concept of Judaism was incarnated through Maccabeen mint symbols. Thus the vessels of divine worship were represented: the wine cup and the festival flowers. What is still missing is the seven-armed candlestick, which a little later was to become the main symbol. The artists took their motives from the nature around them: ears of corn, fig leaves, grapes, and above all the palm tree became symbols.

The art of minting lived through another climax at the time of the Bar Kochba rebellion. Those coins are the most beautiful thing Jewish artists have ever created in that field. They show the Temple itself, its vessels, the amphora and the oil jar, and the musical instruments used by the priests in the Temple. The coins bear inscriptions which have to do with the time of war: "First year of the redemption of Israel." And later on: "For the freedom of Jerusalem." It was always times of suffering which brought the art of minting to its fullest development.

Those were the years when the Jews became conscious of their national essence: that national consciousness called for outer signs and independence. People minted money of their own. Those coins were not merely an outer sign but the representations showed also an inner independence.

Art forms of their own, the inclination towards symbolism and genuinely Jewish criteria — these were to characterize Jewish art for all times from then on.

2

ART AND WRITING

It is not for nothing that the Jews are called the People of the Book. It refers to two things — the people of the Bible and the people of the books.

The Bible, which to the Jews means the Five Books of Moses, the Prophets and the Holy Scriptures, has determined the life and the meaning of the Jews from the very beginning of Judaism to the modern State of Israel.

In the course of time other books appeared — prayer books, commentaries and philosophical works. Even after the invention of the art of printing manuscripts played a role, and except for the Torah scroll they were richly and artfully ornamented. Depending upon their form, all of these manuscripts can be called scrolls, books or single sheets. The scrolls are made of leather or parchment, less frequently of paper. Speaking of their content, we find the following divisions:

The Torah — the Five Books of Moses — is the foremost and holiest basis of the Jewish religion. It is "a tree of life to them that lay hold upon her"

(Proverbs 3:18). The text must be written by hand. The strict laws governing the writing of the Torah scroll forbid ornaments and illustrations. The stern square writing, which is to be measured so that every column contains the same amount of letters, makes a solemn impression. The beauty of the parchment and the relation of the margin to the script are to be considered aesthetic features. Tradition and the loyalty to the Torah created in those scrolls the masterpieces of writing.

The best-known scroll is the Megillah, the Scroll of Esther, which is read during the festival of Purim. This festival is celebrated in gratitude for the miraculous rescue of the Persian Jews by the hand of Esther and Mordecai, at the time of King Ahasuerus. Since the Book of Esther is the only Biblical book in which the name of God does not occur, the scribe could show here all of his artistic abilities in ornaments and illumination. But this was only true if and when the Scroll of Esther was used in the home. In the synagogue, on the other hand, the scrolls had to remain without ornamentation. Usually the Scroll of Esther is placed in a container made of richly ornamented leather, ivory or silver. The writing itself, too, must be mentioned because of its artistic value. The lines of the text are surrounded by a richly illuminated frame. Sometimes the text is not written in columns but within circles or ovals.

The scrolls are accompanied by blessings — sometimes written at the head of the scrolls, at other times on separate sheets — and these blessings, which are recited before and after the reading of the scroll of Esther, show the same artistic treatment as the scroll itself.

Rarely do we find other scrolls. Among these are the Haftara scroll, the Siddur scroll, the Omer scroll and the cabbalistic scroll. They too have certain ornamentation, but they have no special meaning.

Among the Jewish manuscripts which have the form of books are: the Bible, the festival prayer book, the Haggadah, the daily prayer book and other liturgical books, the Talmud, and philosophical works.

Ony a few of the many Bible manuscripts are illuminated. But those few have not only colored ornaments and artistic initial letters but even small drawings and presentations as large as leaves.

The festival prayer book has been created out of a religious need of the Jews. For the prayers, especially those recited during a holiday, became so voluminous that prayer books had to be made. They are richly illuminated and ornamented with various illustrations.

Especially in Italy, Germany and France the art of different epochs is reflected in the illumination and ornamentation of those books. Moreover, prayer books were created for domestic use, and those received very rich decoration.

Just like the Scroll of Esther, the Haggadah is a festival book. It is meant for the holiday of Passover and contains the account of Israel's rescue from Egypt. Again like the festival of Purim, that of Passover has been shaped for the sake of the children, for their enjoyment and their education.

On the first evening of the Passover week, the festival begins with the Seder. The purpose of the Seder ceremony is above all to leave the child with a strong impression. Thus the youngest child at the table asks the question: "Why is this night different from all other nights?" The father then replies by reciting the Haggadah, which is read at home and not in the synagogue. This book has more pictures than any other Hebrew book. We find there many representations, be it from the history of the people of Israel, or from Jewish customs. The Haggadah is the *picture book* of the Jewish home.

Among other manuscripts worth mentioning are volumes of religious prescriptions with glorious illustrations, the book of circumcision which describes that ceremony, and other liturgical books which present religious acts in colorful illustrations.

Philosophical books, too, like Maimonides' *Guide of the Perplexed,* have drawings and rich ornaments.

Single sheets of various sizes served different purposes. There are memorial tablets and prayers, amulets, diplomas and certificates, and above all the richly ornamented Mizrach plaques and marriage contracts (*Ketuboth*).

During their prayers Jews of the Western world turn to the East, and the Mizrach ("East") plaques are meant to indicate that direction. The word Mizrach is in the center of the tablet. The tablets, fixed to the Eastern wall of the synagogue or the home, are paintings or cutouts. They give either a symbolic representation of the city of Jerusalem or the Temple or else scenes of the Old Testament. They are made of paper, metal, leather or stone.

The Ketubot appear as single sheets, too. These marriage contracts are usually written on parchment and decorated in many colors. Often they are masterpieces of writing and of miniature painting. Since the Jews did not have any official registration of births and marriages, in the early times these Ketubot played a major role in family arguments. The marriage contract was concluded by the parties in the presence of two witnesses. The document is framed by ornamental presentations, sometimes also by pictures. It is sometimes complemented by the family's animal signature and weapon.

The invention of the art of printing had a great

influence upon the dissemination of Jewish scriptures, religious as well as secular ones. The oldest Jewish printers came from Italy, where many of the first Italian printing presses were in Jewish hands. Nevertheless the newly imprinted books took over the decorations and illustrations of Jewish manuscripts. The illuminated Haggada books were most frequently printed, as was the Bible. The pictures were mostly woodcuts.

When mentioning Jewish writing we must not forget the gravestones, the most ancient ones of which in Germany are of the eleventh century. Although the inscriptions were very similar to each other, they hardly ever had the same words. At that time the stones were without any ornamentation; only the Hebrew letters bore some kind of embellishment.

Jewish decorative writing can also be frequently found on various domestic or sacred vessels, be they made of metal, wood, ceramics, or textiles. The inscription and the decorations on those objects were almost always the expression of their own epoch.

In the centuries of the middle ages, when almost every book was written by hand, this was not only done for a spiritual enjoyment; it also became a work of art and an aesthetic experience. The number of Jewish illuminated manuscripts of the middle ages is really imposing. The works of Jewish scribes of tenth-century Egypt are of a classical beauty. The drawing is also the text. Plant ornaments frame the writing. The main color is gold, but sometimes we find dark blue and red. Human representations were deliberately avoided.

Starting with the thirteenth century the ornament was transformed into a Moorish style. The branches and the trellis work became thicker and more massive, and the colors were lighter. In Spain we have pictures and text illustrations besides the ornament. The initials end up in colored heads of animals and grotesque creatures. To decorate the margin strange fabulous creatures are sometimes used.

At the height of Gothic art — from the middle of the thirteenth to the fourteenth century — an ornamental background and architectural elements penetrate Jewish manuscripts. Numerous fantastic figures and complicated compositions in the Gothic style are also found in Torah scrolls. The beginnings of some Biblical books especially are provided with such compositions. The first words frequently show a blue color. The letters of Biblical texts are in the form of decorations made of animals and arabesques, and we even find scenes covering entire pages. In the Gothic style we find in Germany human representations, for instance an entire page picturing a bridal couple.

At the turn of the thirteenth century we find especially in France beautiful Bible manuscripts. The decorative elements consist of plants, geometric figures, or comic presentations. One whole page shows a golden menorah against a blue background. On both sides of its stem there are Biblical scenes — Solomon's judgment and the sacrifice of Isaac. Other French Bible manuscripts have the seven-armed candelabra, Aaron's staff, the jar of Manna, angels, the Tables of the Law, the altar, the laver, and vessels used in connection with the offering of sacrifices. Those vessels are overlaid with gold and stand on a black background of parchment. A Bible from Provence shows similar objects. In this instance they are only in gold, and the background is patterned in blue and red.

In medieval France and Spain there are Haggadah illustrations for almost all topics. The most genuine pictures represent Jewish life; they are genre pictures, hitherto unknown. Presentations of the synagogue service, preparations for the Passover and the distribution of Matzah are well observed and executed. Special mention must be made of the Spanish Haggadah of the Seraillero museum. It is of the fourteenth century and artistically speaking it is certainly one of the most valuable of its epoch.

After the Jews had been driven out of Spain, the Italian Jews became their successors in the field of art. In the atmosphere of freedom, that characterizes the blossoming time of Italian art — the Renaissance — the creations of Jewish artists became so Italian in character that, from a Jewish point of

Maimonides, *Guide of the Perplexed,* Barcelona, 1348.

Zodiac, Synagogue of Beth Alpha.

view, they are sometimes colorless. There are hardly any differences between native and Jewish art.

A book of Psalms — a Jewish manuscript from Italy of the fifteenth century — shows us typical Italian Renaissance ornaments: flowers, angels, and birds. The picture itself also adopts the new character according to the time. The picture is firmly held within a frame, space and the scenery are reproduced perspectively, and man is placed in the center. There are no longer any linear drawings or golden backgrounds.

Genuinely Jewish book painting in Germany begins in the second half of the thirteenth century and reaches its climax in the fourteenth century in a festival prayerbook (formerly in the Kaufmann collection). In illuminated Haggadoth too the idea of the German Jews finds its artistic expression. The Haggadah of Darmstadt "is so to speak a type all by itself; it stands between the older Spanish and the latter German ones. It shows neither the Biblical pictures of the South nor the marginal illustrations of the North. Outside of the two purely worldly drawings at the end, which have no immediate connection with the illustration of the text, the full paged pictures as well as the decoration of the initials refer merely to the festival or else they possess a clearly decorative character. Everything is intended to give a solemn and dignified impression, and thus this Haggadah deserves to be called the noblest of all Haggadoth of the early North German period, and the most representative of all." (August L. Mayer.)

The age of the Baroque and the Rococo are best reflected in the Scrolls of Esther. Italian Megilloth of the seventeenth century contain presentations of the Book of Esther, as well as medallions with lions and branches. At the same time middle European manuscripts show scenic presentations of the holy and secular life of the Jews, done in a delightful and popular style.

Although the art of printing had not yet supplanted manuscripts, printed Hebrew books appeared simultaneously adorned with illustrations, and by the sixteenth century it had already become the custom to decorate the title pages of Hebrew books. The art of decorated printed letters developed rapidly, too.

In the modern State of Israel a young generation is continuing the best tradition of graphics, and the Hebrew book experiences a Renaissance.

3

WORSHIP AND ART

In order to have a proper worship service, Jews require the presence of ten adult men. In the room used for such worship there must be certain objects, with which we shall deal now.

The Torah Scroll is found in the Holy Ark. The oldest representations of such Arks are already to be seen on golden tumblers discovered in the Jewish catacombs of Rome. Here we see already two lions opposing each other. They have remained a favorite symbol on various Jewish cultic objects. The oldest extant Holy Ark is from Cairo (thirteenth century). Another one was manufactured for the synagogue of Modena in 1505.

As is the case with all other Jewish cultic objects, the style and the appearance change with the times and places. The Holy Ark, too, thus has the attributes of style of its time of origin and its surroundings. We find frequently lions, a crown, the Tablets of the Law, pillars decorated with leaves and other ornaments. The most impressive Torah Arks were made in the seventeenth and eighteenth cen-

turies. Thus an Ark dating from the beginning of the eighteenth century has on its four corners twisted pillars. It is decorated with flower ornaments and three symbolic crowns.

The Ark, built into the Eastern wall, had to be covered with a curtain, the size of which depended on that of the door of the Ark. There are various colors. On New Year's Day and the Day of Atonement a white curtain was preferred. We found also blue, red, brown, and even green ones, depending on the donor's taste. The motives used have the same variety as the pillars of the Ark: lions carrying the Tablets of the Law, crowns, and sometimes a ram or a unicorn. The curtains, especially the horizontal parts on top, are richly embroidered. Almost always we find the vessels of the Temple, a candelabra, the altar, the Tablets of the Law, and the Ark of the Covenant. The curtains are usually made of brocade or velvet. The embroidering is done with silver and golden threads. A fine example of a Torah curtain is one of the first half of

18

eighteenth century from Germany. It is done of brown brocade with a many-colored pattern of flowers. In addition it has the seven-armed candelabrum and texts from the Book of Psalms.

The Torah is wrapped in a piece of cloth, and covered with a mantle. The latter has two poles on the top so that the rolls can be put through. The mantle, too, is made of brocade or velvet. In the Near East the mantle is substituted by a cover made of metal or wood. Large synagogues have many such mantles of various colors according to the symbols of the holidays on which they are put to use.

Strange silver ornaments are placed on top of the Torah rolls. They are called *rimmonim* (literally pomegranates) ; here the goldsmith could show off the best of his art. Refined, cast and chiselled work, sometimes in connection with precious stones, give them an especially festive appearance. Different countries have developed different forms of *rimmonim*. In the Near East we have the round form, which brings pomegranates to mind, whereas in the West we find the architectural form of a tower. Bells have been added, particularly in Italy.

Above the two *rimmonim* there is often a silver crown, which, while in itself showing architectural features, is decorated with flowers and branches, and sometimes also with birds, animals, and bells. A Torah crown which comes from Vienna (eighteenth century) represents Biblical scenes. The crown is often carried by six lions.

The Torah is almost always decorated with a silver shield, which is held up by means of a silver chain. The basic form of that shield changes with the style of the time. The earliest ones are square, whereas later ones have round or oval endings. The decoration is done in filigree or relief. Besides leaves and branches there are frequently figures or Jewish symbols.

Since the Torah reader must not touch the letters, a pointer is used, the handle of which has various forms. Sometimes it is round, at other times twisted or square; it may be short and thick or long and thin, massive or pierced; often it is overlaid with jewels. The Dutch type is typical for its long and slim form. The German pointers are mostly pierced. Everywhere they are engraved and present a genuine form of artistry.

The Torah scroll is held together by means of a wrap. It is usually a domestic creation and reflects genuine folk art. At first these wraps were embroidered, but since the eighteenth century they have been painted. The decoration shows flowers, arabesques and branches, sometimes also real figures.

Jewish cultic vessels are not only to be found in synagogues but also in the Jewish home. To the Jews the Sabbath, which is introduced by the lighting of the Sabbath candles, is the climax of the week. Lamps suspended above the table served as Sabbath lamps; originally these were in the form of brass rings with small glass jars for the oil and the wick. In the late Middle Ages there developed a starlike type, sometimes decorated plastically. In reality each country developed its own type. In Holland we find long suspended lamps consisting of several parts which are tied to each other by means of chains. In Germany the stem of the lamp was in the form of a three-storied high tower.

The sanctity of the Sabbath is announced by the blessing over vine and two loaves of bread. Such wine cups were mostly made of silver, rarely of other metal or glass. They were always decorated with engravings which corresponded to the style of that time. We also find inscriptions on such cups. The cups had the forms of cylinders, of bells or else they stood on a base.

After the Sabbath sunset the ceremony of *Havdalah* ("separation") is performed. The proper symbol of the *Havdalah* is a sweet-smelling spice which is kept in special spice boxes. The form and furnishing of the spice boxes enable the artist to develop his entire imagination. The form of the box varies so much that it comprises the fauna, the flora and even the world of technology. For several centuries, starting with the Middle Ages, the overwhelming majority of spice boxes kept to the form of a tower. They have often different stories, and sometimes they are so naturalistic that one imagines one recognizes definite structures. At times there are also human representations. The boxes are made of silver. Often we find extremely precise filigree work, which is particularly true of Italy.

In addition to the Sabbath the Jews celebrate other festivals, which lead to the use of various vessels and objects. The Passover festival, which recalls the Exodus of the Jews from Egypt, begins with an evening on which the entire family partakes of a meal (*Seder*). Every place at the table has its own wine cup, made of glass or silver. The table is covered with a special Seder cloth, and the Matzoh lie on the so-called Matzoh plate. These plates are made of silver or tin. The plate reflects representations of Biblical scenes and persons from the Old Testament. The rim shows fruit and branches. Some Seder plates portray a Passover meal in a popular style.

Another Jewish holiday which is connected with the home is Chanukka (Feast of Dedication or of Lights). The Talmud states as follows: "On the 25th day of Kislev is the beginning of the Chanukka festival. It consists of eight days, and it is forbidden to mourn or to fast. The basis for the festival is the following event: When the Syrians entered the Temple by force, they desecrated its oil supply. When the Hasmoneans had solidified their victory and the Syrians had been defeated, they found, after a long search, one single little jar which had been sealed with the seal of the High Priest. It contained oil for one single day. But a miracle occurred, and it burnt for eight days. In the following year those days were instituted as holidays with songs and praises." The climax of the Chanukka festival is the kindling of the lights. On the first night one light is kindled, and one is added each night as the week proceeds.

From the very beginning Chanukka candelabra have been domestic vessels. In the early Middle Ages a type of wall candelabrum developed. In the Middle Ages and during the Renaissance the back wall had the form of a triangle. Later centuries loosened the form through volutes, etc., and the back wall has already become an oval or square form. They are made of silver or other metals. Medieval sources tell us also of Chanukka candelabra in the synagogues. They were meant for the strangers and the poor, who could not celebrate the holiday at home. This called for a larger type, and therefore the seven-armed Menorah was used. That type was subsequently introduced into the home too.

The French Chanukka candelabras of Gothic times show window roses and Gothic pillars in the middle of the wall triangle. In Italy the decorations became increasingly richer. We find armorial lions, Renaissance vases and rich ornaments. The free-standing Chanukka Menorah is often found in Germany. It is decorated with angels' heads and crowned with flowers and bells, in addition to animals in relief. The Menorah often ends up in a representation of Judith with the head of Holofernes.

During the Purim festival friends send each other fruit and Purim cake. For these gifts special plates are used, called Purim plates. Most of them are made of tin. The mirror of the plate shows portrayals from the Book of Esther or other ornamental decorations.

Other Jewish customs and ceremonies too are closely connected with the religion and require special vessels. The circumcision is performed by a qualified man who uses a special knife. These knives, which are sharp on both sides, have a handle made of rock-crystal, jasper, sometimes of ivory, more rarely of metal. The handle is carved or engraved; the sacrifice of Isaac is a favorite motive. Thus the handle of a circumcision knife which dates from seventeenth-century Italy shows the sacrifice of Isaac. The entire knife is done in the style of early baroque.

The Jewish marriage ceremony has its own special form. The wedding, performed by a rabbi, takes place under the Chuppa (canopy). The climax of that ceremony is the handing over of the ring. Jewish wedding rings belong to the most precious in this type of art, the traditional form having been maintained for centuries without a change. Ever since the Renaissance filigree and granulation have been preferred. Often the rings show a small house as a symbol of the new home or that of the Temple. The rings are made of gold and contain ornaments of enamel, and are often provided with lions' heads and inscriptions reading *Mazal tov* (Good luck). The bride wears a bridal girdle made of various strands. It is often decorated and has small engraved silver plates.

Among the Jewish population who lived around the Mediterranean and in the Near East it was quite customary to wear amulets. They were not only worn as a protection from misfortune, sickness and the "evil eye," but also as an ornament. On Jewish amulets, which were mostly of silver, we find the word Shaddai engraved. Sometimes they are written on parchment and kept in special containers. Such containers are the work of the art of engraving, and the execution shows the style of their period. In the homes of pious Jews a small scriptural scroll is fixed to the upper part of the doorpost. This is called a Mezuza. It is placed in a capsule of metal or wood, which is either simple or richly decorated. It is supposed to protect from sin. Only one word of the text is visible in the capsule; this is the word Shaddai, which means Almighty. The containers are of various forms — a small structure with an open gable, others have an architectural fragment surrounded by columns, and sometimes they are topped by lions or crowns.

In the course of the centuries the Jew could express his sense of the beautiful only in an art which served his religion, and thus the works of religious artistry did not have the purpose of being pure art, but they were the expression of the praise of God, just as had been the case of the lyre and the Psalms of that great artist of the Jewish people, King David.

4

PAINTING

Post-exilic Jewry, driven out of their homeland, existed only as a community of faith. In the diaspora the Jews went on living as an organic unity which grew and relied on the soil of the traditional instructions and customs, whether they had been handed down orally or in writing. The meaning of Jewish life during the millennium of the State was to be found in the relationship to God, and this goal was responsible for the life form out of which arose a civilization with all its branches, like art, ethics and tradition. But living among strange peoples and civilizations influenced the Jewish people so strongly that they did not always remain loyal to their law but yielded to their surrounding culture. They did not always abide by the commandment: "Thou shalt not make for thyself an image of what is in the heaven above or on the earth below or in the water underneath the earth."

As mentioned above, the Jews were driven out of Jerusalem after the Bar Kochba rebellion. They went first to the countries around the Mediterranean, and there we find the first traces of Jewish art, part of which is painting.

One of the first testimonies of Jewish painting in the first centuries A.D. is to be found in the Jewish catacombs in the vicinity of Rome. Those wall paintings do not differ from neighboring non-Jewish ones. In the Jewish catacomb of Torlonia one finds a representation of an Holy Ark between two seven-armed candelabra or the lighted Menorah and to the right and left of it pomegranates and a horn. Those are definitely Jewish symbols. In the second Jewish catacomb of Vigna Randanini one already encounters representations which have nothing to do with Judaism. A winged goddess of victory crowns a young man; a rooster, a lamb, peacocks, but also a falling Menorah are shown there. Jewish and pagan elements and symbols are intermingled. The formal division of the ceiling and the walls in circles and squares corresponds exactly to the general style of catacomb painting of those days.

The House of God — the Temple of Jerusalem

— had been destroyed by the Romans; and, having emigrated to many countries, the Jews began to erect houses to their Lord. The first synagogues of post-exilic Jewry — in Palestine as well as in other countries around the Mediterranean — looked for their architecture to the style of their days. The synagogue of Dura Europos (in modern-day Syria) was conquered and destroyed by the Persians in the third century A.D., but the excavations permit us to admire the synagogue frescoes which remain.

Those frescoes represent events and figures of the Old Testament. Nor is there a lack of Jewish symbols: a Menorah with its accessories and the Temple. Of special interest, however, are the group scenes which portray a prophetic vision. The prophet addresses the elders of the exile. The resurrection of the dead leaves a mighty impression. The contrast of the colors make an imprint on the viewer. Later synagogues — from the fourth to the seventh centuries — were decorated with mosaics, which here too refer to Biblical tales and Jewish symbols. Their light colors were also intended to illuminate the synagogues and fill them with glory and festivity. The synagogue of Beth Alpha is particularly impressive through its colorful mosaics. In the center of the mosaic we see the zodiac, and in its center the sun god Helios is seen in his chariot. The other fields of the mosaic are devoted to the sacrifice of Isaac, the Holy Ark with lions, and the Menorah. Other objects too are visible.

Another mosaic of the synagogue of Aegina shows patterns in the form of a carpet. A finely done ornament and the precise division of the fields give an example of a well-thought-out composition.

As was the case with other peoples, the Jews of the Middle Ages also employed painting for their manuscripts. The great creations which the Jews displayed in this field have been dealt with in the chapter on Art and Writing. But as an example I would like to mention two manuscripts which are paintings rather than illuminations. A German festival prayerbook of the fifteenth century is decorated with very original miniatures. The painting is done in a rather popular style, but very charming because of the light colors and the lively type of story-telling. The second example — the Book of Psalms — is also of the fifteenth century, but this time from Italy. One of the decorated pages of the work shows four small fields portraying scenes from the life of King David. In this case, however, it seems that the artist was not Jewish, since the king's pose is a Christian one. Nevertheless the illumination done during the Italian Renaissance belongs to the Jewish circle. As a matter of fact up to the time of the Baroque manuscripts were the main painting done by Jews, although there is in addition another kind of painting.

The wooden synagogues of Eastern Europe were painted in light colors, with plant ornaments and animal pictures. Some wooden synagogues in Germany show similar features. One example is the prayer room of the congregation of Horb. On wooden beams at the Western wall there is a medallion, carried by two lions who blow trumpets. The center group is flanked by a city with many towers — supposedly Jerusalem — on the one side, and on the other a fruit basket with palm branches. On the ceiling there are Baroque flowers and fruit arabesques in addition to animals and birds. It is a beautiful example of popular Jewish painting.

Up to the emancipation we have commissioned art. In more modern painting, when art was persued for art's sake, the Jewish element is not so evident any longer in the works of Jewish painters.

Thus Israels was a genre painter as were others of his time. Liebermann's pictures are to us typical for German impressionism. His art is first of all German — just as that of the impressionist Pissaro is first of all French. The pictures of the Italian Modigliani, with their imitation of the Gothic style, are as little Jewish. They symbolize the loneliness of modern urban man, be he Jewish or non-Jewish.

There are some Jewish painters who do choose Jewish topics for their pictures, but their style, form and color do not differ from those of other artists.

Contrary to such Jewish painters Marc Chagall

is completely and visibly Jewish. He is a type by himself, who never belonged to a certain school. In his paintings the same elements reoccur again and again, although in ever-changing forms: the couple in love, a watch, a horse, a cow, goats, fish, birds, a street in Vitebsk, the seven-armed candelabrum, the Rabbi, and the Torah scrolls.

In these paintings the laws of gravity are done away with, as well as those of central perspective and causality.

In his autobiography Chagall wrote: "I try to create a world in which everything is possible, where there is no reason to be surprised at anything nor for stopping to be surprised." What is reflected here is the world picture of the Hassidim, who are characterized by a joy in the world as it exists, and also a joy in wondrous tales.

At the same time impressions from the artist's childhood come here to the fore, and that childhood had been spent in a believing Jewish home, surrounded by those who shared the same faith.

This unique art of painting has been called sur-naturalism by Guillaume Apollinaire. It is said that this word created the subsquent term surrealism. But the surrealistic paintings known to us are not similar to Chagall's. His is a unique style, which is not shared by any other painter of his time.

When he was told of the persecutions of the Jews, the crucified Christ appeared more and more often in his paintings. This Christian figure, often wearing a green soldier's cap, and placed side by side with Jewish elements — the rabbis and the seven-armed candelabrum — is to him a symbol of human suffering.

Perhaps in the phenomenon of Chagall there is something miraculous which characterizes the history of Jewish creative art. As has been mentioned previously, in times of the greatest danger to the Jews, when their physical and spiritual existence was at stake, something genuinely Jewish found expression in their art.

REPRODUCTIONS

Reconstruction of a cultic place at Hazor, fourteenth to thirteenth century B.C.

Stele with hands from Hazor.

Canaanite goddess from Naharia. Form and cast.

Scarabs from Ginossar (Genezareth). Period of the Hyksos.

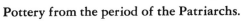

Pottery from the period of the Patriarchs.

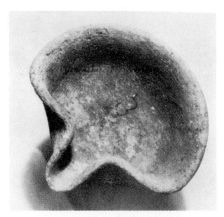

Oil lamp, period of Patriarchs.

Censer made of chalk. Megiddo, beginning of first century B.C.

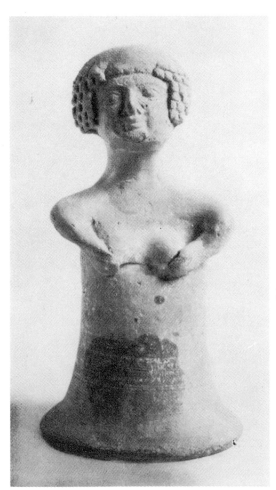

Idol of Astarte. Eighth to seventh century B.C.

Capital from Ramath Rachel. Ninth to eighth century B.C.

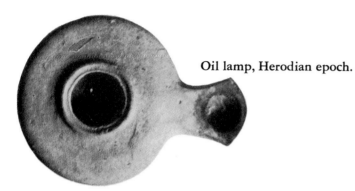

Oil lamp, Herodian epoch.

Pot, Herodian epoch.

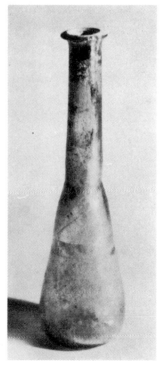

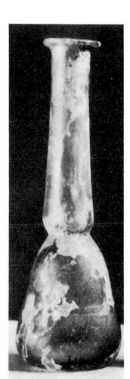

Balsam flasks, Herodian epoch.

Jewish and Roman coins 68–69, and 132–135 A.D.

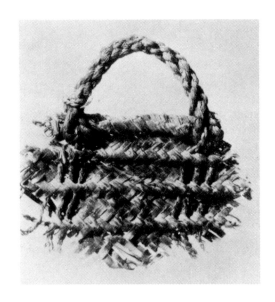

Parts of a linen garment, a sandal and a hand basket. Period of the Bar Kochba rebellion, found at Nachat Chever.

Ossuaries, made of stone, Herodian epoch.

Jewish coins. 1st and 3rd row: coins from the time
of the Bar Kochba rebellion 132–135 A.D. 2nd and
4th row: coins from the years 68–69 A.D.

Bible, Provence (?), 1301.

Title page of the festival prayer book, Worms, Germany.

Jewish and Roman coins 68–69, 132–135 A.D.

Holiday prayer book Spain, thirteenth century.

The seven-armed candelabra Rome, Arc of Titus.

Handwritten facsimile of the Isaiah scroll.

Bible, Germany, 1290.

Bible, 1298.

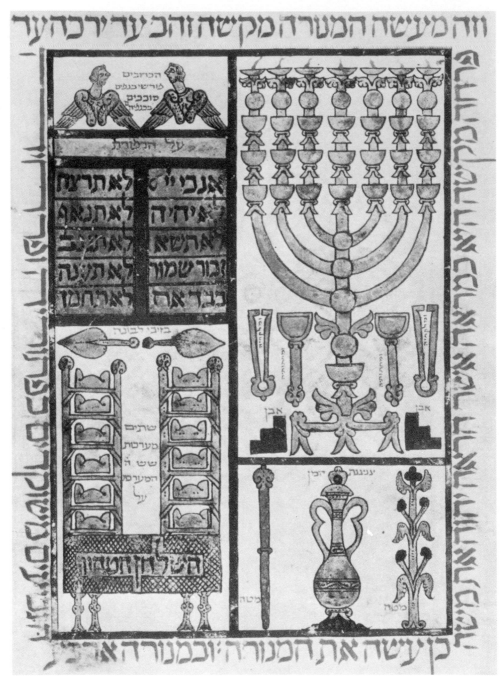

Bible, Perpignan, 1299.

Bible, France, 1300.

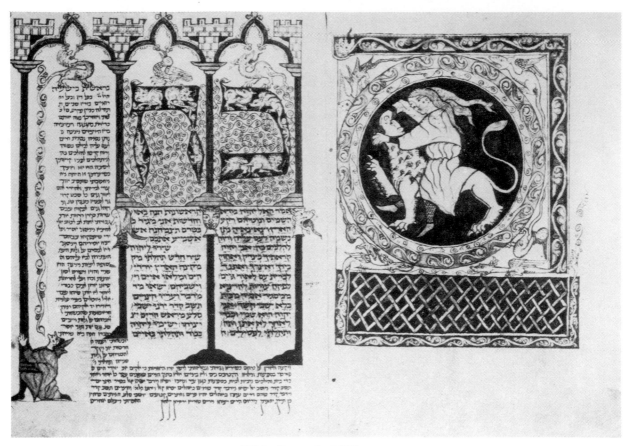

Bible, Brussels, 1310.

Holiday prayer book, Germany around 1300.

Bible, Spain, fourteenth century.

Bible, Bohemia, fourteenth century.

Bible, Germany, fourteenth century.

Holiday prayer book, Spain, fourteenth century.

45

Bible, France, fourteenth century.

46

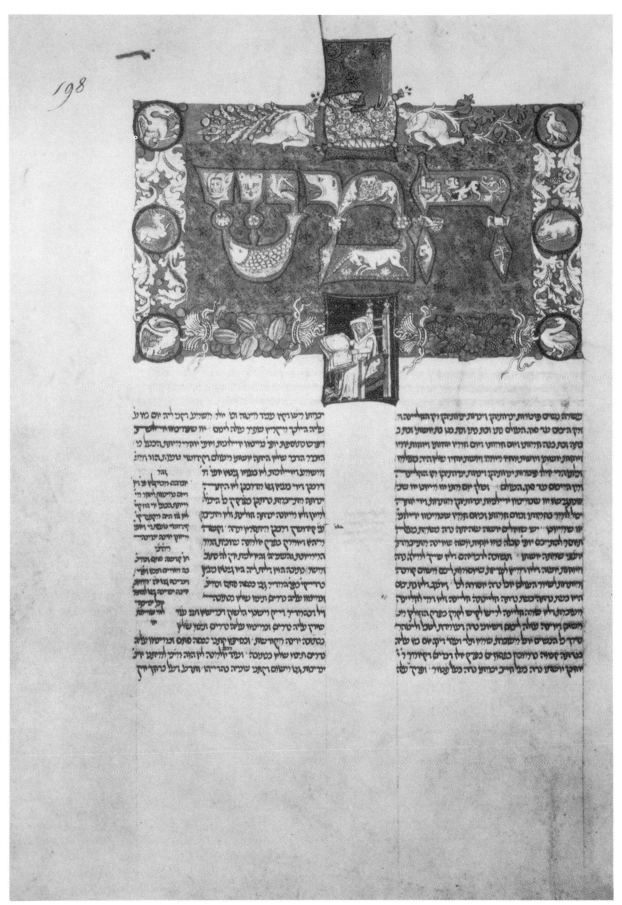

Commentary on the Talmud, fourteenth century.

Bible, Germany, fourteenth century.

Haggadah, Germany, beginning of fifteenth century.

Bible, Germany, fourteenth century.

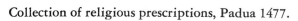
Collection of religious prescriptions, Padua 1477.

50

Scroll of Esther, Italy or Southern France, around 1600.

Liturgical book, Germany, 1590.

Seder haevronot, Bingen (Germany), 1649.
Scroll of Esther, Italy, seventeenth century.

Scroll of Esther, Netherlands or France, about 1700.

פֶּסַח · מַצָה · וּמָרוֹר :

פֶּסַח שֶׁהָיוּ אֲבוֹתֵינוּ אוֹכְלִים בִּזְמַן שֶׁבֵּית הַמִּקְדָּשׁ
קַיָּם · עַל שׁוּם מָה · עַל שׁוּם שֶׁפָּסַח הַקָּדוֹשׁ
בָּרוּךְ הוּא עַל בָּתֵּי אֲבוֹתֵינוּ בְּמִצְרַיִם · שֶׁנֶּאֱמַר וַאֲמַרְתֶּם
זֶבַח פֶּסַח הוּא לַיָי אֲשֶׁר פָּסַח עַל בָּתֵּי בְּנֵי יִשְׂרָאֵל בְּמִצְרַיִם
בְּנָגְפּוֹ אֶת מִצְרַיִם וְאֶת בָּתֵּינוּ הִצִּיל וַיִּקֹּד הָעָם וַיִּשְׁתַּחֲווּ :
מַצָה זוּ שֶׁאָנוּ אוֹכְלִים · עַל שׁוּם מָה · עַל שׁוּם
שֶׁלֹּא הִסְפִּיק בְּצֶקֶת שֶׁל אֲבוֹתֵינוּ לְהַחֲמִיץ
עַד שֶׁנִּגְלָה עֲלֵיהֶם מֶלֶךְ מַלְכֵי הַמְּלָכִים הַקָּדוֹשׁ בָּרוּךְ
הוּא

Haggadah, Breslau, 1768.

Scroll of Esther, Central Europe, end of eighteenth century.

Circumcision book, Hungary, 1819–20.

Gravestone of Zippora, Speyer, 1113.

Gravestone of Hannah, Speyer, 1121–22.

Gravestone of the boy Israel, Regensburg, 1282.

Gravestone of Meshullam, Mayence, 1171.

Gravestone of Jacob, Würzburg, 1339.

ravestone of a young martyred woman, Speyer,
:ond half of the fourteenth century.

57

Marriage contract, Modena, eighteenth century.

Memorial stone of the burial society, Altona, seventeenth to eighteenth century.

Marriage contract, Yemen, 1795.

Gold bottom of a tumbler, Rome, third to fourth century A.D.

Bernhard Picart, 1673–1733: Holy Ark.

Holy Ark, Vienna, 1707.

Crown of a Holy Ark, Franconia, about 1740.

Torah curtain, Rhineland, beginning of eighteenth
century.

Torah curtain, Germany, 1729.

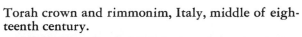

Torah mantle, Germany, nineteenth century.

Torah container with rimmonim, Iraq, 1904.

Torah crown and rimmonim, Italy, middle of eighteenth century.

64

Haggadah, Germany, beginning of fifteenth century.

Torah shield, silver, partly gilded, with half jewels.
Nurnberg, about 1700.

Rimmon, France, middle of eighteenth century.

Rimmon, Amsterdam, 1769.

Rimmon, Persia, nineteenth century.

Rimmon, Frankfurt, beginning of eighteenth century.

Rimmon, Poland, middle of eighteenth century.

Torah crown, Vienna, middle of eighteenth century.

Torah crown, Germany, middle of eighteenth century.

Torah crown, Austria, middle of eighteenth century.

Torah shield, Poland, 1736.

Torah shield, Warsaw, second half of eighteenth century.

Torah shield, Central Europe, eighteenth century.

Torah shield, Frankfurt, beginning of eighteenth century.

Torah shield, Frankfurt, beginning of eighteenth century.

Torah shield, Vienna, eighteenth century.

Torah shield, Nürnberg, beginning of eighteenth century.

Torah pointer, Hamburg, 1771.

Torah pointer, Amsterdam, 1754.

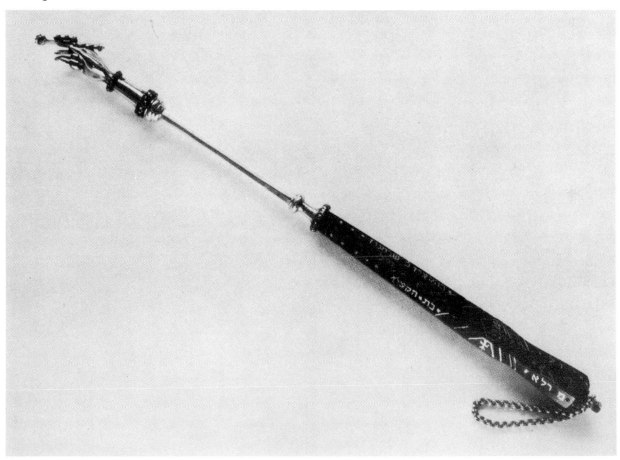

Torah pointer, Warsaw, second half of eighteenth century.

Torah pointer, Galicia, eighteenth century.

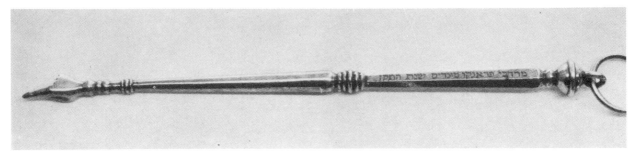

Torah pointer, Holland, 1790.

Torah pointer, Poland or Galicia, eighteenth century.

Torah pointer, probably Germany eighteenth century.

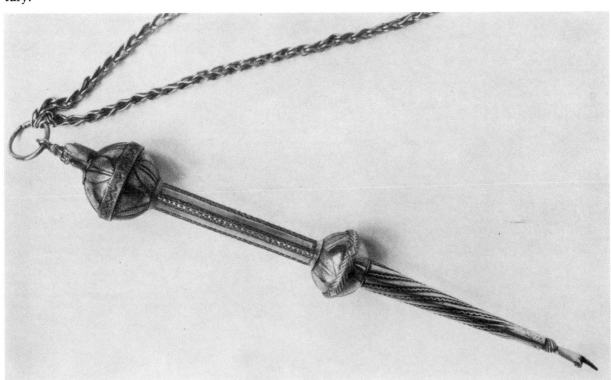

Torah wrap, Ulm, 1736.

Torah wrap, Germany, 1738.

76

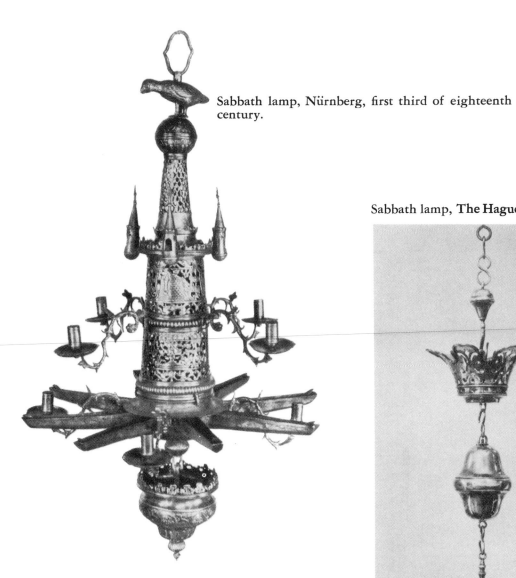

Sabbath lamp, Nürnberg, first third of eighteenth century.

Sabbath lamp, **The Hague**, 1764.

Kiddush cup, Persia, eighteenth century.

Kiddush cup, Nürnberg, about 1700.

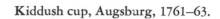

Kiddush cup, Augsburg, 1761–63.

Kiddush cup, Augsburg, about 1710–15.

Spice box, Frankfurt, middle of eighteenth century.

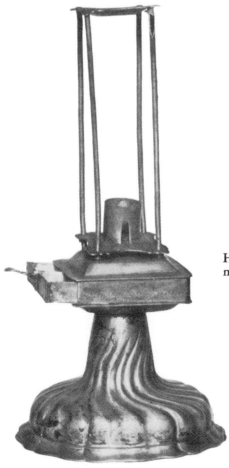

Havdala candle holder with spice box, Nürnberg, middle of eighteenth century.

Spice box, Hamburg, middle of eighteenth century.

Spice box, Nürnberg, end of seventeenth century.

Torah wrap, linen with silk embroidery, southern Germany, 1731.

Chanukka Menorah, Frankfurt, beginning of eighteenth century.

Spice box, Germany, second half of eighteenth century.

Spice box, Danzig, end of seventeenth century.

Spice box, Poland, nineteenth century.

Spice box, Eastern Europe, nineteenth century.

Seder cover, Germany, about 1800.

Seder plate, Germany, 1788.

Same, 1748.

Seder plate, Germany, eighteenth century.

Passover cup, Vienna, 1858.

Seder plate, Germany, 1787.

Seder plate, Holland, eighteenth century (?).

Seder plate, Persia, nineteenth century.

Chanukka Menorah, Southern France, twelfth century.

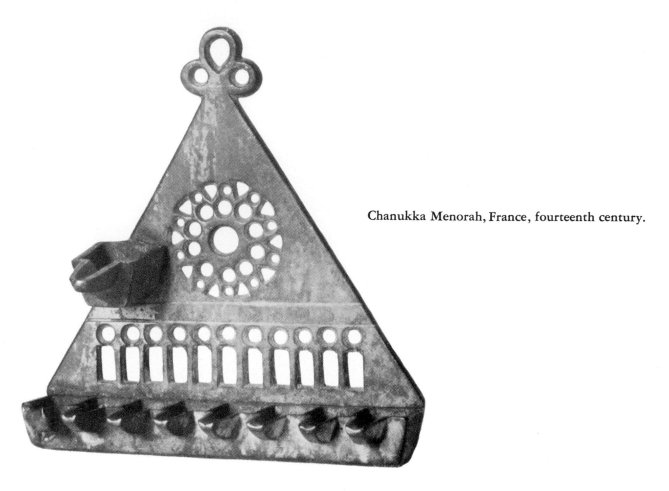

Chanukka Menorah, France, fourteenth century.

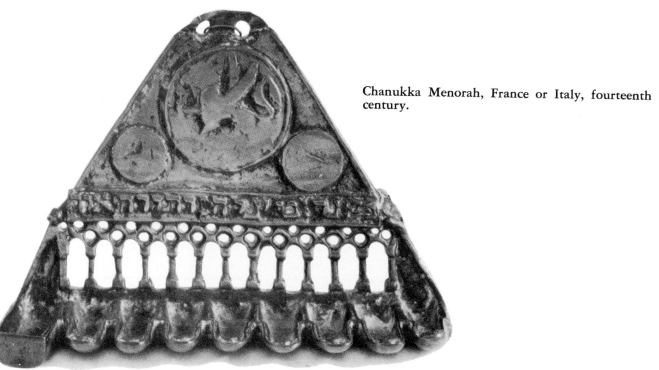

Chanukka Menorah, France or Italy, fourteenth century.

Chanukka Menorah, Jerusalem, eighteenth century.

Chanukka Menorah, Holland, eighteenth century.

89

Chanukka Menorah, Poland, eighteenth century.

Chanukka Menorah, Italy, sixteenth century.

90

Chanukka Menorah, **The Hague**, beginning of eighteenth century.

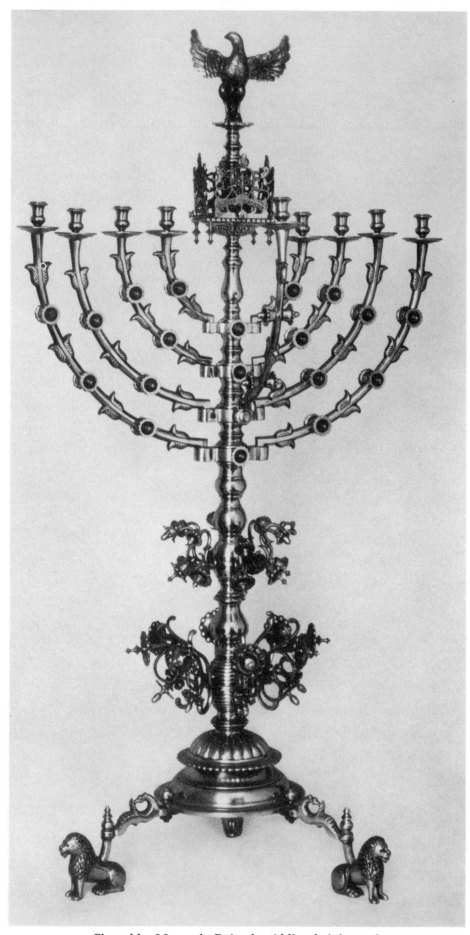

Chanukka Menorah, Poland, middle of eighteenth
century.

Chanukka Menorah, Frankfurt, second half of eighteenth century.

Chanukka Menorah, Poland (?) eighteenth or nineteenth century.

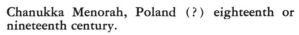

Chanukka Menorah, Southern Germany (?),
eighteenth century.

Chanukka Menorah, Frankfurt, 1666–1681.

Purim plate, Germany, 1753.

95

Circumcision knife, central Europe, seventeenth or eighteenth century.

Same, Italy, seventeenth century.

Scroll of Esther in silver container, Italy (?) eighteenth century.

Circumcision knife, Northern Germany, seventeenth century.

Spice box, Italy, eighteenth century.

Sabbath afternoon by Moritz Oppenheim, 1800–1832.

Sand bowl, Venice, seventeenth century.

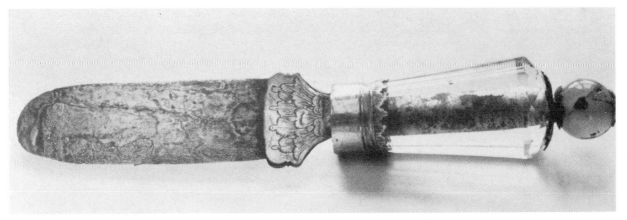

Circumcision knife, Germany, eighteenth century.

Silver plate, Galicia, beginning of nineteenth century.

Wedding rings, Italy, sixteenth century.

98

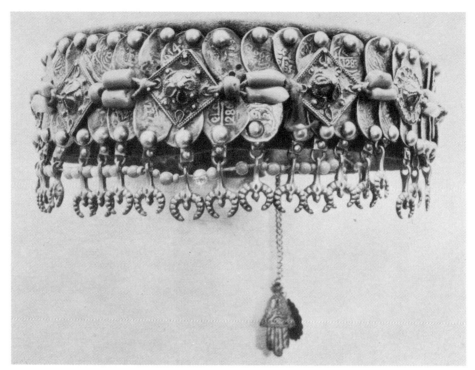

Bridal crown, Morocco, nineteenth century.

Bridal girdle, Frankfurt, 1658–1678.

Amulet container, Venice, seventeenth century.

Shaddai amulet, Italy, eighteenth century.

Amulet container, Italy, beginning of eighteenth century.

100

Mezuzah, Eastern Europe, eighteenth century.   Mezuzah, Poland, nineteenth century.

Amulet, Persia, eighteenth century.

Wall painting: Holy Ark between two seven-armed candelabra. Catacomb of Torlonia, Rome.

Horn, candelabrum and pomegranate on ceiling of above catacomb.

102

Painted room, catacomb of Vigna Randanini,
Rome.

Moses reading from the Torah. Dura-Europa, Synagogue.

Exodus from Egypt.

Consecration of the Tabernacle. Synagogue of
Dura-Europos.

The vision of Ezekiel, synagogue of Dura-Europos.

The Ark of the Covenant in Philistia. Synagogue
of Dura-Europos.

The vision of Ezekiel. The resurrection of the
dead. Dura Europos.

Eagle above Medusa's head. Synagogue mosaic, Yafia.

Mt. Gerizim between two seven-armed candelabra, Samaritan synagogue, Shaalbim.

Holy Ark, candelabra with accessories, synagogue
mosaic, Jericho.

Seven-armed candelabrum and accessories, mosaic,
Naro (Hamman-Lif, Tunisia).

Mosaic with inscription, synagogue, Aegina.

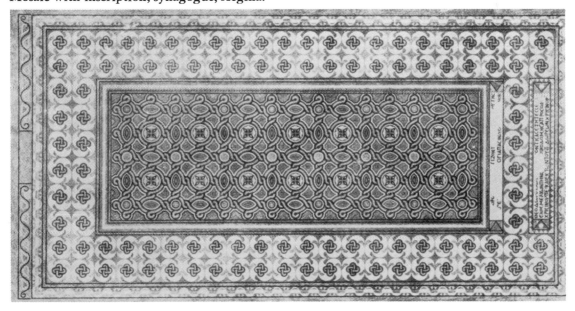

Ram and wild ox, synagogue, Yafia.

Holiday prayerbook, Germany, before 1427.

The Book of Psalms, Italy, fifteenth century.

112

Studying the Talmud. Isidor Kaufmann, oil on wood.

Rabbi with Torah scroll. Marc Chagall.

Jewish house of prayer, Horb. Eliezer Zusman ben Shlomo Katz, 1735.

Rabbi, reading. Joseph Israels, 1824–1911.

Old Jew. Etching by Hermann Struck, 1876–1944.

Synagogue in Paris. Colored chalk on paper and
cloth by Edouard Brandon, 1831–1897.

Illustration to Heine's *Rabbi of Bachrach,* by Max Liebermann 1847-1935.

Jewish Wedding, by Joseph Israels, 1824–1911.

Jews Mourning in Exile. Oil on cloth. E. J. F. Bendermann 1811–1889.

Purim Players, Jankel Adler, 1895–1949.

Man Praying. Jacob Steinhardt, 1887–1968.

Susanna and the Elders. Lovis Corinth 1858–1925.

Rabbi. Zendel.

Jewish Wedding. Issacher Ryback, born 1897.

120

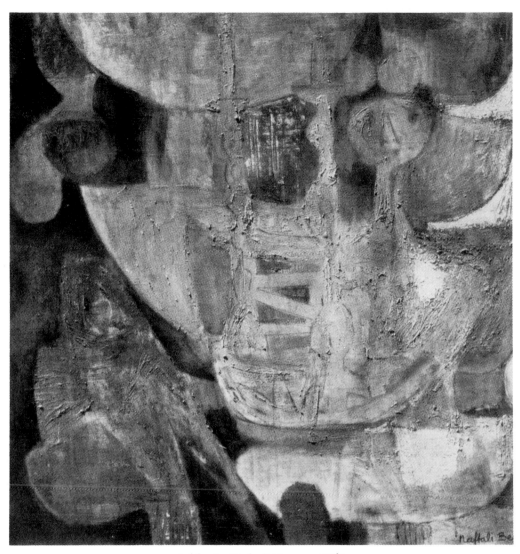

Sabbath. Naftali Bezem, 1960.

Rabbi. Hap Grieshaber, born 1909.

Man Praying. Ludwig Meidner, born 1884.

122

Man and Child. Mane Katz, born 1894.

Succoth Festival. Shmuel Bonneh, 1960.

The Synagogue. Marc Chagall, born 1889.

Rabbi. Marc Chagall.

Rabbi. Marc Chagall.

The synagogue of Safed. Marc Chagall.

The Yellow Rabbi. Marc Chagall.

SHORT BIBLIOGRAPHY

1 Cohn-Wiener Ernst   *Die Jüdische Kunst.* Berlin 1929

2 Frauberger Heinrich   *Verzierte hebräische Schrift und jüdischer Buchschmuck* in Mitteilungen der Gesellschaft zur Erforschung jüdischer Kunstdenkmäler. Frankfurt am Main V—VI, 1909

3 Frauberger Heinrich   *Über alte Kultusgegenstände in Synagoge und Haus* Mitteilungen der Gesellschaft zur Erforschung jüdischer Kunstdenkmäler. Frankfurt am Main 111—IV, 1903

4 Goodenough E. R.   *Jewish Symbols in the Grecco-Romain Period.* New York 1953

5 Kanael Baruch   *Die Kunst der antiken Synagoge.* München-Frankfurt 1961

6 Kaufmann David   *Gesammelte Schriften.* Frankfurt am Main 1915

7 Landsberger Franz   *Einführung in die Jüdische Kunst.* Berlin 1935

8 Naményi Ernest   *La Miniature Juive au XVIIe au XVIIIe Siècle.* Revue des Etudes Juives XVI, 1957

9 Reifenberg Adolf   *Denkmäler der jüdischen Antike.* Berlin 1937

10 Roth Cecil   *Die Kunst der Juden.* Frankfurt a. M. 1962

11 Stassof Vladimir   *L'Ornement Hebreu.* Berlin 1905

12 Steinschneider Moritz   *Vorlesungen über die Kunde hebräischer Handschriften.* Jerusalem 1937

13 Synagogakatalog   *Katalog der Ausstellung.* Recklinghausen-Frankfurt 1960/61

14 Wischnitzer Rachel   *The Messianic Theme in the Paintings of the Dura Synagogue.* Chicago 1948

15 Wischnitzer-Bernstein Rachel   *Symbole und Gestalten der Jüdischen Kunst.* Berlin-Schöneberg 1935